It's Not Fair!
¡No es justo!

by Rebecca Gómez
Illustrated by Roberta Collier-Morales

SCHOLASTIC INC.

New York   Toronto   London   Auckland   Sydney
Mexico City   New Delhi   Hong Kong   Buenos Aires

For my own beloved siblings: Stewart, Karen, Jonathan, and David.
—R.G.

To Jorge, who I learned so much from.
—R.C.M.

No part of this publication may be reproduced in whole or in part, or stored in a retrieval system, or transmitted in any form or by any means, electronic, mechanical, photocopying, recording, or otherwise, without written permission of the publisher. For information regarding permission, write to Scholastic Inc., Attention: Permissions Department, 557 Broadway, New York, NY 10012.

ISBN 0-439-61644-1

Text copyright © 2004 by Rebecca Gómez.
Illustrations copyright © 2004 by Roberta Collier-Morales.

All rights reserved. Published by Scholastic Inc.
SCHOLASTIC and associated logos are trademarks and/or registered trademarks of Scholastic Inc.

12 11 10 9 8 7 6 5   8 9/0

Printed in the U.S.A.
First printing, January 2004

It's winter vacation.
Charlie should be happy.
There's no school for one week.
But Charlie isn't happy, he is mad!

Llegaron las vacaciones de invierno.
Charlie debería estar contento.
No hay clases durante una semana.
Pero Charlie no está contento, ¡está
enojado!

Mamá takes two children to Mexico
every year.
Liliana and Charlie went last year.
Charlie loves Mexico.

Mamá lleva a México a dos de sus hijos
cada año.
Liliana y Charlie fueron el año pasado.
A Charlie le encanta México.

Mamá, Luis, and Pilar are going to
Mexico to visit family this year.
Charlie will be left behind.

Mamá, Luis y Pilar van a ir a
México a visitar a la familia este año.
Charlie se tendrá que quedar en casa.

Charlie won't have anything to do.
Liliana will be busy with her friends.
Papá will be at work.
Charlie will be with Abuela all day.

Charlie no tendrá nada
que hacer.
Liliana estará ocupada
con sus amigas.
Papá se irá al trabajo.
Charlie se quedará en
casa todo el día con la
abuela.

It *is* Luis and Pilar's turn to go.
Charlie still thinks it's not fair.

Les toca ir a Luis y Pilar.
Charlie sigue pensando que no es justo.

Abuela says, "Don't worry, Charlie.
We'll do fun things."
Luis says, "Don't be mad, Charlie.
I'll call you every day."

La abuela le dice:
—No te preocupes, Charlie. Nos divertiremos mucho.
Luis le dice:
—No te enojes, Charlie. Te llamaré todos los días.

Charlie doesn't want to be left behind.
Why can't Mamá take three children
this year?
Sometimes it is hard to be the little
brother.

Charlie no quiere quedarse en casa.
¿Por qué este año mamá no puede
llevar a tres niños?
A veces no es fácil ser el hermano
menor.

"Mamá, can't I come, too?" he asks
again.
Mamá says, "Don't worry, Carlitos.
You'll go again next year."
She hugs him and kisses him.

—Mamá, ¿no me puedes llevar a mí también? —pregunta otra vez.
Mamá le dice:
—No te aflijas, Carlitos. Volverás a ir el próximo año.
Ella lo abraza y lo besa.

Luis tries to make Charlie feel better.
"Let's go outside and play," he says.
They are out in the snow all day.
Luis and Charlie build a giant snowman.

Luis trata de animar a Charlie.
—Vamos a jugar afuera —le dice.
Juegan en la nieve todo el día.
Luis y Charlie hacen un muñeco de
nieve gigantesco.

There is a big surprise when they
come back inside.
Liliana and Pilar have been working
in Charlie and Luis's bedroom.

Se llevan una gran sorpresa cuando
regresan a la casa.
Liliana y Pilar han estado trabajando
en el dormitorio de Charlie y Luis.

"Surprise!" they shout when Charlie walks in.
Charlie can't believe it.
There are bright lights all around the room.

—¡Sorpresa! —gritan cuando Charlie entra.
Charlie no lo puede creer.
Hay luces brillantes por todo el cuarto.

Abuela's colorful serape is tacked to
the wall.
There are maracas on the shelf.
A Mexican flag and a United States
flag now hang on the wall.

El sarape de colores de la abuela está extendido en la pared.
Hay maracas en el estante.
Una bandera mexicana y una bandera de Estados Unidos cuelgan ahora en la pared.

There are postcards from Mexico taped to the mirror.
"This is great!" Charlie says. "It's almost as good as going. Thank you!"

Hay postales de México
pegadas en el espejo.
—¡Qué maravilla! —dice
Charlie—. Es casi tan lindo como
viajar. ¡Gracias!

Mamá cooks a special feast for dinner.
Luis tells Charlie to look out the
kitchen window.
Charlie opens the curtains.
Wow!

Mamá prepara una comida especial
para la cena.
Luis le dice a Charlie que mire por la
ventana de la cocina.
Charlie abre las cortinas.
¡Guau!

Charlie sees their big snowman.
Luis has given him one last surprise.
Now he is wearing a giant sombrero!

Charlie ve un gran muñeco de nieve.
Luis le da una última sorpresa.
¡El muñeco tiene un sombrero gigante!

Charlie smiles.
He hopes the snowman never melts.
Sometimes it *is* good to be the little brother!

Charlie sonríe.
Espera que el muñeco de nieve nunca se derrita.
¡A veces tiene mucho de bueno ser el hermano menor!